THURMOND
A New River Community
Ken Sullivan

PREFACE

Among those who have contributed to this short history of the town of Thurmond, my first thanks goes to William Eugene Cox, former Chief of Interpretation at the New River Gorge National River. From the National Park Service's early days in Fayette County, Gene laid the groundwork for a comprehensive historical accounting for the territory within the bounds of the National River, doing much of the initial research himself. The idea for this book and others in the series was his, and he mothered the first ones through to completion.

Neil DeJong, another steady Park Service professional, took up where Gene Cox left off, inheriting me and my book at first-draft stage. Former National River Superintendent Jim Carrico, while taking no direct hand in the project, made it possible that such work could go forward by his recognition of the important place of history among the Park Service's other responsibilities within the New River Gorge.

Others include my colleague in this series, Professor Lou Athey of Franklin-Marshall College, the source of much good New River conversation over the years. Major Thomas W. Dixon of the Armed Forces Staff College provided information on railroading and directed me to photographs, as did Eugene Huddleston of Michigan State University; both are affiliated with the remarkably well-organized Chesapeake & Ohio Historical Society.

Finally, I thank Jack Kelly, Jacqueline Pugh, Jane Graham Lawson, Wallace Bennett, Bill Hickman and others who shared their personal knowledge of Thurmond. They and their neighbors living and dead have eased the historian's burden considerably by living a story so interesting that it was a genuine pleasure to write.

--Ken Sullivan

Thurmond's lower end as it appeared in 1986. The large house here was featured as the boarding house in the movie *Matewan.* Photo by Doug Chadwick.

CONTENTS

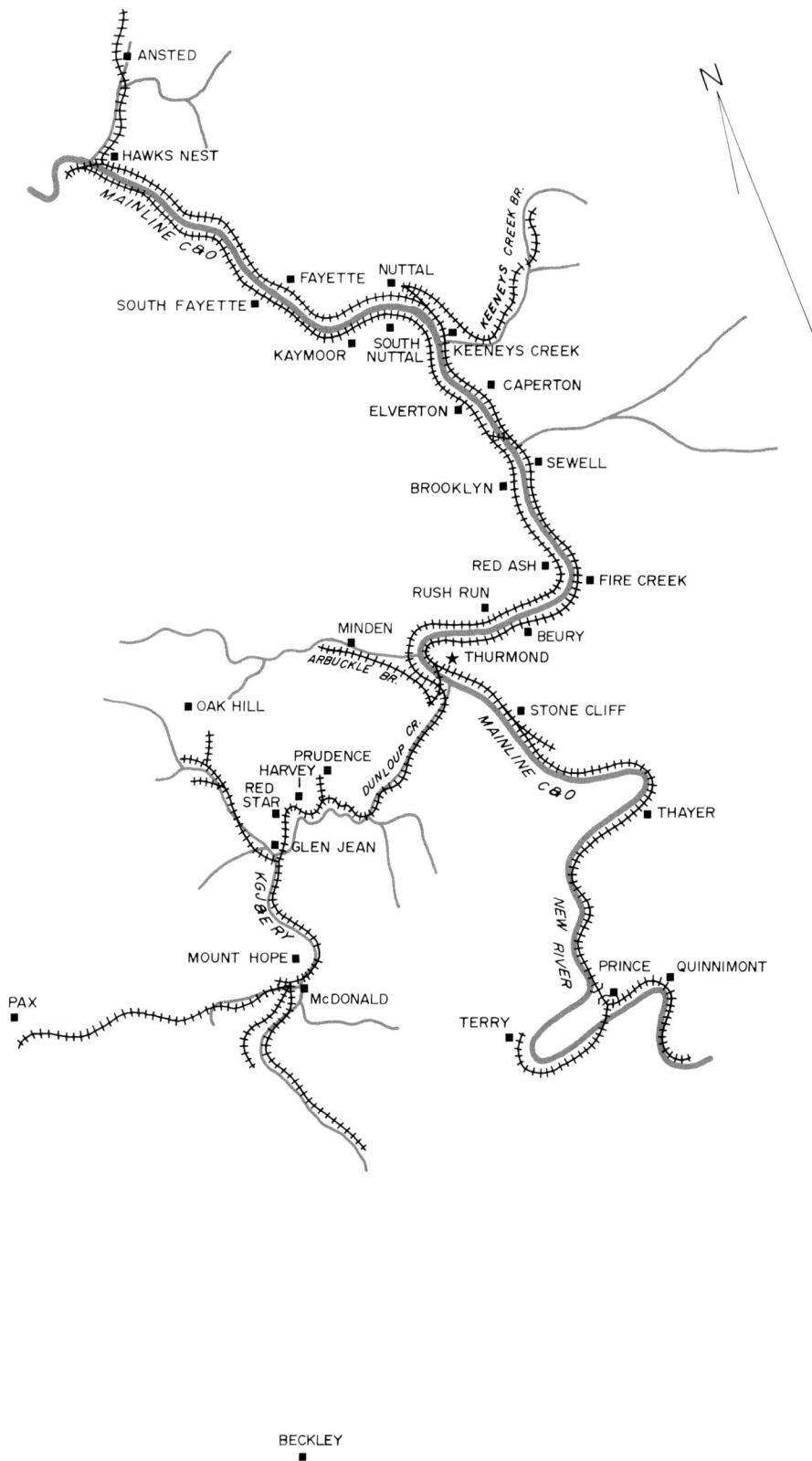

ANSTED

HAWKS NEST

MAINLINE C&O

FAYETTE

NUTTAL

SOUTH FAYETTE

KAYMOOR

SOUTH NUTTAL

KEENEYS CREEK

KEENEYS CREEK BR.

CAPERTON

ELVERTON

SEWELL

BROOKLYN

RED ASH

FIRE CREEK

RUSH RUN

BEURY

MINDEN

ARBUCKLE BR.

THURMOND

OAK HILL

STONE CLIFF

PRUDENCE

HARVEY

DUNLOUP CR.

RED STAR

GLEN JEAN

MAINLINE C&O

THAYER

K G J & E RY

NEW RIVER

MOUNT HOPE

PRINCE

QUINNIMONT

PAX

McDONALD

TERRY

N

BECKLEY

Thurmond, principal rail lines, and the surrounding area as they appeared early in the century.

vi

Captain William Dabney Thurmond, late in life. Until age 89, "he rode his horse wherever in the county his business called or his pleasure inclined him," according to a *Fayette Tribune* story following his 1910 death. Photo by William O. Trevey, date unknown, from the collection of Bill Hickman.

INTRODUCTION

Thurmond is the heart of West Virginia's New River Gorge, a legendary town concocted about equally of the determination of a former Confederate ranger leader and of geography and the economics of railroading and coal mining. Captain William Dabney Thurmond and the Chesapeake & Ohio Railroad appeared within a few months of each other in early 1873. The C&O was completing its east-west main line, and the Captain was the new owner of the site that would provide for a time the most lucrative town on the railroad's entire system.

Thurmond lies in one of several great curves that the New River has made in cutting its gorge through the Fayette County plateau. It is not a promising site, with a steep mountain immediately behind, the river in front and very little level land in between. But geography was kind in other ways. On the outside of the big river bend, opposite the town, Dunloup and Arbuckle creeks wind down from the mineral-rich southern plateau. The two streams offer natural routes into the gorge, opening the way for millions of tons of coal to come to Thurmond.

Captain Thurmond had lived in the neighborhood long enough to recognize the advan-

1

tages of the location. As a young man he had come across the mountains from Amherst County, Virginia, settling with his father's family on Arbuckle Creek in the early 1840's. His sentiments remained with the South during the Civil War, and as the leader of Thurmond's Rangers he made a fearful reputation among local Unionists. When his house was torched by enemy troops in 1863, Thurmond moved his family away from Fayette County until several years after the war. By the early 1870's he had rebuilt at Minden, taking up his pre-war work as a farmer and self-taught surveyor.

In 1873 Thurmond was commissioned by John Bowyer to survey land on the north side of New River. Cash was scarce and he agreed to take his pay in 73 acres of land. His acreage was more rugged than the rest of the original tract, but he was mindful of the two creeks across New River. The new railroad was on Thurmond's side of the river and if coal ever traveled down Dunloup and Arbuckle for shipment to market, it must cross at a point on or very near his land. Trains would have to be made up at the junction, equipment serviced and the needs of railroad men attended to. It seemed likely that money could be made at such a place.

Financially, the Captain's dreams worked out largely as planned. Within 30 years his rocky river bend had become a bustling rail center, writing his surname indelibly into the history of West Virginia. The town of Thurmond became a major shipping point on the C&O, in some years supplying more than twice the freight tonnage and revenue of Cincinnati and Richmond combined. Captain Thurmond shrewdly retained ownership of almost all his land and added the rest of the original Bowyer tract to it, providing an economic base for launching generations of his family into industrial leadership in the state.

But in other ways the town was a bitter disappointment. The bearded, hawknosed Thurmond was an upright Baptist, unaccepting of weakness in himself or others. Nonetheless,

the town became notorious for the vices the man himself eschewed, making the proud family name synonymous with rambunctiousness for the better part of a century. This fact galled Thurmonds at least until the Captain's grandson's time. Family members pointed out that the lawlessness occurred in areas technically outside the town and beyond the stern patriarch's control, and that the reputation of the place was at any rate exaggerated. Their protestations were largely in vain.

Thus, Thurmond in its heyday was a town of contradictions. It thrived on the serious and respectable business of making money in a new industrial era, yet acquired the popular reputation of an outlaw community. Within the city limits Captain Thurmond's rules and the C&O timetable were both strictly observed, but sin flourished on the doorstep. Gambling, prostitution and hard drinking were common, with violence their occasional companion. Most of the licentiousness occurred across New River and legally within the boundaries of the town of Glen Jean, but that distinction was lost on casual onlookers. The Thurmond area was known as the place for a good time in the hardworking coalfields, and all recognized the the fun might be legal or illegal and its consequences possibly deadly.

The contradictions have never been resolved. Thurmond is mostly a ghost town now, with both the good and bad of its youth long behind it, but the legend of the place has grown proportionate to its physical decline. Ironically, this legend, so baneful to Captain Thurmond in his lifetime, is in part the basis for a modest revival of his town. Geography remains important, also. As always Thurmond is a natural gateway to the gorge, now providing access to the recreational resources of the New River Gorge National River rather than to the buried wealth of a great coalfield. The boom times haven't returned but the town of Thurmond is again making money, prospering today from tourists drawn by the wild history of the place and the wild river that flows by.

CHAPTER ONE

"An Important Point on the Road"

Development, 1873-1910

Railroading and coal mining came together in a spectacular way at Thurmond, birthing the town and accounting for most of the later history of the place. The coal had always been there, buried in the surrounding mountains and exposed for easy driftmouth mining wherever stream erosion cut through the strata of the geologic layercake. The rails came in 1873, when the Chesapeake & Ohio Railroad snaked its main line down the New River. This is the treacherous gorge section of the New, and at first sight seems an improbable route for a major transportation artery. In fact, however, the river had operated according to the unerring principles of nature in finding the least resistant passage through the hard rock of the surrounding plateau. The resulting canyon provided an efficient, low-grade route of the sort sought eons later by railroad engineers.

The advantages of such an east-west commercial corridor had long been apparent, although earlier hopes had hinged on plans to make the river itself navigable. The dream of opening the New to traffic was an old one, dating from the abortive James River and Kanawha Canal project of George Washington and other early Virginians. This ambitious scheme proposed to link the James at Richmond to the Kanawha River by a series of canals, thus connecting eastern Virginia to the rich trade of the Ohio Valley.

The New River from the mouth of the Greenbrier to the head of the Kanawha was an essential link in this plan. These 64 miles from Hinton to Gauley Bridge present a 700-foot fall in elevation, however, and a rapidly flowing river, particularly in the final section. Commissioners sent out by the Virginia Assembly in 1812 found this part of the proposed canal route to be "an almost continued succession of shoals and falls," further noting the "steepness, cragginess and abruptness of the banks." In many places prospects for navigation were nothing less than "awful and discouraging," the report soberly pointed out, in words not likely to be disputed by novice rafters tackling the unruly river today. Virginia's canalization hopes foundered against such obstacles, but plans to improve navigation on the lower New River were put forth as late as 1872.

In that year further canal plans were rendered forever obsolete, as the C&O advanced through the New River country. The rail line dubbed itself "George Washington's Railroad," in part following the proposed canal route through the mountains. Predecessor railroads had pushed as far west as Clifton Forge, Virginia, before the Civil War halted construction. Work resumed after the war, and the C&O followed tributaries of the Greenbrier River into the new state of West Virginia in 1869.

Railroad building in the mountains was arduous work, with the contracting companies said to bury a "man and two mules" for each mile of track. The legendary John Henry

3

Fine brick banks are the mark of a prospering community. The National Bank of Thurmond, the town's second bank, first opened for business in the Hotel Thurmond in 1906. This picture is from a later period. Photographer and date unknown, from the New River Gorge National River collection.

himself met his death on the West Virginia C&O line, in an heroic battle against a new steam drill at the Great Bend Tunnel on the Greenbrier. The worst working conditions were encountered within the New River Gorge, where construction gangs labored among sandstone cliffs in the hard winter of 1872.

Still, the work pushed ahead. While track crews built westward from Virginia, others worked eastward from the Ohio River. The rails were joined at Hawks Nest, 18 miles below Thurmond, on January 29, 1873. That night a special train pressed on to Huntington, West Virginia's new city named for C&O president Collis P. Huntington. There a barrel of James River water was poured into the Ohio, signifying the realization of Washington's dream of joining East and West. It was at this auspicious time that Captain William D. Thurmond entered the scene, acquiring his New River acreage on April 1 of the same year.

Completion of the C&O opened the way for

development of the New River Coalfield, the first of southern West Virginia's famous "Smokeless Coalfields." Mineral speculation and some preliminary mine work had preceded the railroad, and at Quinnimont Colonel Joe Beury was standing by to ship the first New River coal soon after the railroad was put into service. Other pioneer operators quickly followed, and by 1880 coal was also being mined at Nuttallburg, Ansted, Fire Creek, Elm Station, Hawks Nest and Sewell. The high quality local coal was especially valuable for coke making and an alliance was struck with the iron industry of western Virginia. Within a few years, gas-belching beehive coke ovens lined the tracks near the new coal mines.

The town of Thurmond did not share in this earliest chapter of New River industrial history. The coal that came rolling over the new tracks had no reason to pause at Captain Thurmond's property, and for several years the place had no more significance than any other point on the Chesapeake & Ohio main line. Its importance came only with the building of the railroad bridge and the opening of Dunloup and Arbuckle creeks by branch railroads, and the locating of C&O yards and shops. Mining was not undertaken at Thurmond and, unlike other communities springing up along the river, it never became a coal company town.

Thus Captain Thurmond at first found himself with a townsite and no town. The upper half of the New River Gorge remained mostly wilderness during these years, marked only by the shining ribbon of steel rails. It was 1878 before a post office was established at River View, on the north side less than a mile above Thurmond's land. This was the first post office in the 16-mile stretch between Quinnimont and Fire Creek. A railroad station was established at River View at about the same time.

The initial returns to the Captain were modest and more in keeping with the area's agricultural past than its industrial future. His first local venture was a New River ferry just above the mouth of Arbuckle Creek. Soon heavy wagons passed his home at Minden, winding their way down Arbuckle to the river and the railroad. They carried lumber and the produce of the countryside for shipment to the new coal towns in the gorge and tobacco for the market in Richmond, returning with outside commodities for merchants in Oak Hill and other plateau communities. The Captain's flat-boat, carrying a single wagon and team at 20 cents per trip, made as many as 15 trips daily in good weather, according to his grandson. A rowboat supplemented the larger craft, carrying pedestrians at a nickel apiece. Mail also crossed at the Thurmond ferry, on its way from

The New River railroad bridge made Thurmond a major coal shipping junction and therefore "an important point on the road," in the words of Charles Thurmond. The bridge was built in 1887-89 and this photo made sometime after 1901, when the Dunglen Hotel, visible at rear, was constructed. Photo by William O. Trevey, from the collection of Bill Hickman.

Above: **Track side elevation, Thurmond depot.** From C&O Railway Passenger Station plans.

Below: **The railroad intersection was the heart of Thurmond's prosperity. Coal cars crossing over from Dunloup Creek and the south side joined the C&O main line here, after being made up into trains at the Thurmond yards. The depot and freight station are to the left of the bridge, with the Dog Wagon food stand on the near side of the tracks.** Photographer unknown, about 1915. Courtesy C&O Historical Society.

C. & O. RY. SHOPS AND YARDS, THURMOND W. VA.   Pub. by C. E. Armstrong

Postcard view of Thurmond repair shops and rail yards, about 1910. Hurvitz and Lopinsky's Leader store, at right, advertised dry goods, a complete millinery department under the direction of Miss Pearl Robinson, and "coffins and caskets of all sizes" in a 1908 issue of the *Fayette Tribune*. Photographer unknown, courtesy C&O Historical Society.

the C&O up to Oak Hill. The ferry operated at least until 1888, but was displaced by the railroad bridge which opened a year later.

By this time Thurmond's riverbend tract had been permanently occupied, his son Joseph building the first small house there in 1884. In 1887-89 the railroad bridge was built 100 yards upstream from the Thurmond land, running diagonally across New River to the mouth of Dunloup. A southside branch line, initially serving the Thurmond Coal Company mine near Arbuckle Creek, was built at roughly the same time as the bridge. The building of the Dunloup Creek branch, constructed as a joint venture by the C&O and land baron Thomas G. McKell in 1893, opened up a more important mineral hinterland to Thurmond. The first carload of Dunloup coal rolled down from Collins Colliery at Glen Jean late that fall, with many thousands more to follow.

The bridge and branch lines assured the proposed town's future as a strategic rail junction. "This bridge makes this an important point on the road," W. D. Thurmond's son Charles ob-

served confidently in early 1888, while construction was under way. So it did, and the family's speculation began to pay off. A freight depot was established about the time the bridge was begun, and construction of rail yards on Thurmond's land occurred at the time of the building of the bridge. The first store, owned by Captain Thurmond and Oak Hill merchants Charles T. and George W. Jones, with Charles Thurmond in charge, was opened. The Thurmond family began building houses, rental units ranging in size from four rooms to as many as eight or ten. The frame dwellings, eventually numbering 30 or more, were scattered wherever perches could be found, especially along the tracks west of what was to be the central business district and on the mountainside above.

The community was named during this busy period, with postal authorities officially designating "Thurmond" for the post office established in the Jones and Thurmond store. Local stories have it that Captain Thurmond himself preferred to retain the railroad name of Arbuckle, but that was unacceptable since

7

Soon after the turn of the century, Thurmond included (left to right) the Armour meat house, the big Hotel Thurmond and a three-story commercial building, with the Mankin Building closing out the main business block. The building later occupied by the National Bank of Thurmond will fill the gap by the hotel. Photo by William O. Trevey, date unknown, from the collection of Bill Hickman.

there was already a post office of the same name in West Virginia. According to grandson Walter R. Thurmond, the old man later maintained that "the boys," his sons, proposed the family name without his knowledge. However it happened, that was the name on the successful application submitted to the Post Office Department in February 1888. Storekeeper Charles Thurmond began handling the mail as Thurmond's first postmaster in 1889.

The riverside town grew steadily over the next decade. Population was estimated at 75 by 1895-96. There were at least a half-dozen businesses, including Western Union, Adams Express, two general stores and the offices of two coal companies. By 1898 estimated population had more than doubled, to 175. Thurmonders now enjoyed the services of one more store, a restaurant and a nearby saloon, as

well as two milliners, a lawyer, shoemaker, jeweler and photographer. Scotsman Thomas Scott was in charge at the Hotel Thurmond and H. O. Nichols had set up as barber. Law and order were represented in the persons of Constable J. W. Bragg and Justice of the Peace Clay Workman.

Thurmond bustled by the turn of the century. The overall level of business remained about constant, but there were several newcomers among the town's enterprises. W. S. Parkinson and Company had opened a drugstore, and Farm and Water Produce had set up as the community's first wholesale distributor. Captain Thurmond's 1891 frame hotel building had burned in 1899, to be replaced by an impressive 35-room brick hotel opening at the beginning of 1902. The new three-story building boasted seven bathrooms, steam heat, and 400

8

electric lights powered by its own generator. The hotel lobby, kitchen and a dining room seating 60 occupied the second floor, with a drugstore, general store and Nichols' barbershop among several businesses on the ground level below.

While the new Hotel Thurmond was taking shape in 1901, a more difficult building job got under way across the river. Railroad construction crews moved into daunting terrain to begin an Arbuckle Creek branch line for coal operator W. P. "Paddy" Rend's Minden mine. Meanwhile, the C&O went to work to build more side tracks opposite Thurmond on the south side. Rend's grade ran high along the canyon wall above, at one point sliding massively to cover the lower C&O tracks to a depth of 30 feet or more. The completion of the Arbuckle Branch in 1904 rounded out Thurmond's rail network, adding an essential link that would eventually convey a million tons of coal a year to the town by the river.

In 1901 the community also acquired the fabulous Dunglen Hotel, the institution that set the social tone of Thurmond during the prime years. The hotel was across the river by the south end of the bridge, on land belonging to Thomas G. McKell. McKell, the area's leading landholder, built the 100-room hotel as a local showpiece. He imported hotel manager Alden Pence Butterfield from Cincinnati and brought in an orchestra from Columbus for an opening night ball. "Butterfield ran her high, wide, and handsome," in the words of a contemporary, and life was gay at the Dunglen from then on. The hotel bar reportedly never closed from 1901 until state prohibition took effect in 1914, parties were frequent and high-stakes gambling continued nonstop. The New River Gorge had seen nothing like the Dunglen, nor has it since.

The freewheeling ways of the Dunglen Hotel and of the more unsavory establishments that sprang up around it were not to be tolerated on Captain Thurmond's own land. Their presence nearby was among the reasons for the incorporation of the Town of Thurmond in 1903, with son Joseph S. Thurmond as first mayor. Incorporation provided for a degree of governance exceeding that of mere ownership, and certain controls -- including a veto over the licensing of saloons -- could be exercised over adjacent unincorporated areas. The McKell family countered with the extension of the legal boundaries of the town of Glen Jean all the way down Dunloup Creek, protecting the liquor license of the Dunglen. The riverside community was now split into two legal entities, with the halves at moral odds with one another.

The standoff did not inhibit development.

J. H. GRUBB
Jeweler and Optician :: Silverware

Musical Instruments, Watches, Diamonds, Eastman Kodaks and Photo Supplies. Repairing of all kinds a specialty. C. & O. Watch Inspector.

Thurmond - - West Virginia

Jeweler J. H. Grubb appeared in Thurmond by 1902 and did business there for many years. This 1906 advertisement indicates that he helped keep the trains on time as an official C&O watch inspector. From the *Official Industrial Guide and Shippers' Directory*, C&O Railway, 1906.

The McKells, Glen Jean and Thurmond's Reputation

Thomas Gaylord McKell, Captain W. D. Thurmond's neighboring landowner, was lord of the rich Dunloup Creek mineral basin. McKell, born in Chillicothe, Ohio, in 1845, married into West Virginia coal in 1870. His bride, Jean Dun of the Dun and Bradstreet Duns, brought a part interest in 12,500 acres of undeveloped Fayette County land to the marriage. After inspecting the property, McKell bought out the other owners in the tract, and increased it through purchases to an eventual 25,000 acres. McKell's land extended generally throughout the Dunloup Creek drainage, from the headwaters down to the mouth and on across New River to a-

Thomas Gaylord McKell owned southside Thurmond, including the Dunglen Hotel. Gambling and drinking flourished on his side of the river. Photographer unknown, from the collection of George Bragg.

but the eastern boundary of Captain Thurmond's much smaller riverbend property.

The development of McKell's vast holdings depended upon transportation for the underlying coal. The Chesapeake & Ohio main line was constructed down New River opposite Dunloup Creek in 1873. The completion of the Thurmond bridge in 1889 brought the tracks to McKell's side of the river. The wealthy landowner then arranged with the railroad company for the building of the Dunloup branch line, finished in 1893. These rails opened the bulk of the estate to mining, initially undertaken by leaseholders on the McKell lands.

T. G. McKell died in 1904, succeeded by his son William. The younger McKell was born in Chillicothe in 1871, but chose to make his home at Glen Jean after his graduation from Yale. Bill McKell was a powerful man of great wealth and strong opinions. He is still vividly remembered by older residents of the area as a tight-fisted man who was nonetheless generous on several particular occasions and who lavished time and money on his company softball team. Following an early disappointment in love -- his imported fiancee is supposed to have surveyed Glen Jean from the depot and inquired whether it would be necessary for her to live there, whereupon Bill replied in the negative and loaded her back on the train, alone-- McKell remained a lifelong bachelor, immersing himself in business and Republican politics.

Glen Jean served as local headquarters for the McKell ventures. The town was founded by T. G. McKell in the mid-1890's and gratefully named for his wife. The heart of Glen Jean lies at the confluence of Dunloup and White Oak creeks, just off present U.S. 19. In incorporating the town, however, the

William McKell, millionaire bachelor, inherited his father's vast mineral holdings on Dunloup Creek. Here he pauses at work in his Glen Jean office, about 1935.
Photographer unknown, from the collection of George Bragg.

elder McKell extended its legal boundaries to the mouth of Dunloup, and on across New River to adjoin Thurmond on the east. Lower Glen Jean developed in conjunction with the town of Thurmond and the technical distinction between the two was unapparent to casual observers.

This fact was to have a profound effect on local history and on the reputation of Thurmond. The McKells did not share the moral zealousness of W. D. Thurmond, and their domain became a haven for diversions forbidden in the Captain's town. T. G. McKell built the legendary Dunglen Hotel at his end of the Thurmond bridge in 1901. Neither he nor his son are known to have disapproved of the hotel's use as a gambling center, and Bill McKell was accused of harboring a variety of worse vices nearby. *The Whiskey Ring*, an anonymous pamphlet put forth in the heated county political campaign of 1912, charged that McKell profited knowingly from prostitution and other illegal activities carried on in rental properties he owned. The pamphlet's vengeful author concluded that Bill McKell "for the love of money, had led his fellow man into vice and debauchery."

The anonymous pamphleteer particularly had in mind the "Ballyhack" district of lower Glen Jean, at the mouth of Dunloup diagonally across from Thurmond proper.

Ballyhack was home to the notorious Black Hawk, Stackalee, South Side and other watering holes of questionable repute. In these places "short skirt" dances might be enjoyed, skin and crap games partaken of, and whiskey and the favors of women purchased by those inclined to spend the money and endure the dangers. While it is unlikely that Bill McKell took any direct role in the affairs of these dives, such places would not have survived the direct opposition of him or his father.

Nor could such places have survived a lack of demand for the services they provided. Southside Thurmond was a rare free zone within the New River Coalfield, not subject to the iron rule which coal operators imposed on surrounding company towns nor to the morals enforced by the Thurmond family within the corporate limits of Thurmond. When miners, railroaders and traveling men wanted to blow steam, Ballyhack was one of the few places available to them. Even the good citizens of Thurmond proper sometimes needed an outing, according to contemporary resident Virginia Mankin. "The best people would get fed up, and as outlet, would go across the river and get drunk," she recalled in a later interview. Mrs. Mankin's observation suggests a more complex relationship than simple antagonism between prim Thurmond and its dark twin across the river.

11

The Mankin Building marked the city limits, with everything to the right being officially in the town of Glen Jean. J. Ward Mankin was a doctor and druggist and a major civic leader during Thurmond's boom years. Photo by William O. Trevey, after 1910, from the collection of Bill Hickman.

Thurmond boomed following incorporation. The Captain turned loose a little over an acre of land in three building lots in 1903 -- all he would part with before his death, aside from a school lot and railroad rights-of-way -- and the real estate fetched record prices. Armour and Company paid a middleman $90 a front foot for its first narrow lot near the Thurmond Hotel, reportedly the most ever paid in Fayette County. Armour would be a major local enterprise over the next 30 years, shipping wholesale meats up and down the railroad and attesting to Thurmond's primacy as a distribution center.

In the same year, 1903, young Dr. J. Ward Mankin arrived to practice medicine, soon establishing himself as a local business and professional leader. His red brick Mankin Building, completed in 1904, remains a Thurmond landmark today. Black Davy Mitchell, depot food vendor and train announcer, appeared at about the same time as Mankin. Harrison Ash was on the payroll as police chief, and Glen Jean mayor Leo Schaffer had opened a general store in the riverside community. After Captain Thurmond and Bill McKell, Mankin, Mitchell, Ash and Schaffer were Thurmond's great names, and by 1904 this colorful cast of characters was all in place.

The new C&O depot was opened in 1904, replacing an earlier structure lost to fire in 1903. Across the river on the south side, the New River Banking & Trust Company, later one of Dr. Mankin's tenants, was formed in August 1904, under the direction of Bill McKell and several important local coal men. The community acquired its second financial institution, the Thurmond Bank (later the National Bank of Thurmond), two years later. This Thurmond family institution first opened for business inside the Thurmond Hotel, but soon built the neighboring bank building that in recent years has housed the Bankers Club hotel and restaurant. This commercial boom of the town's busiest decade essentially gave central Thurmond its final shape, and by 1910 a tight row of proud brick facades fronted on the "main street" of the Chesapeake & Ohio Railway.

Good roads contributed to Thurmond's undoing, lessening the region's dependence on railroads. Here a Koehring Paver surfaces a bridge on the Dunloup road at upper Glen Jean. Photo by William O. Trevey, date unknown.

CHAPTER TWO

"Good Roads and a Bad Name"

Maturity and Decline

Captain William D. Thurmond died in May 1910. His 90 years had spanned a critical period for the United States, dangerous times when American nationhood was tried by the fire of war before emerging triumphant. The civil conflict split Thurmond's native state, making an involuntary West Virginian of him. He was never fully reconciled, refusing the national oath of allegiance following the Civil War and naming a succession of saddle horses for Confederate heroes. But like the railroad building planters of Faulkner's novels, the aging Captain accommodated himself to a key change in the postwar nation, the emerging industriali-

Postcard view of the Thurmond depot. The freight station and bridge may be glimpsed at right. Photographer and date unknown, from the New River Gorge National River collection.

Thurmond's economy was geared to the needs of steam locomotives. Those days were almost over when No. 1051 pulled out with the Keeney's Creek mine run in September 1954. Photo by Gene Huddleston, courtesy C&O Historical Society.

zation of the South. The town of Thurmond was not his only gambit in the new age, for he did well leasing family mineral lands around Arbuckle Creek, but it was a major element in his success.

The Captain's town was not to enjoy so long an ascendancy as had the man himself, but that would not have been apparent in 1910. Thurmond was moving more than 200 people a day through its new train station and making more money for the railroad than any other place on the line. Indeed, the station would have to be expanded within five years, to provide more waiting room and more baggage room. The community was entering its robust prime, and things looked as if they might continue that way indefinitely. All in all, it was a good year for the founder to take his leave.

Thurmond, as an incorporated place, was seven years old in 1910. It participated in its first national census as a separate political entity that year, reporting a population of 315 people. When census taker Owen Amick made his rounds in April, he found a hard-working community with nearly 150 townspeople gainfully employed. The largest single group - more than 60 -- were railroaders, but there were also retail clerks, barbers, bookkeepers and insurance agents, among others, at work in the busy town of Thurmond. Charles and Joseph Thurmond were both present to look after the founding family's interests, listing themselves with the census enumerator as real estate men.

Greater Thurmond had two banks during this period, as well as the Chesapeake & Potomac Telephone exchange for the entire region, the local Western Union office, two doctors, two fine hotels, various restaurants, stores of different kinds, and two churches battling the notorious saloons outside the city limits. Several coal sales agencies directed the outflow of the local product, while Armour and other wholesalers facilitated the arrival of goods from the outside. The Dunglen kept a special showroom for the benefit of nonresident wholesalers, where traveling drummers might display their wares for the merchants who flocked in from miles around. Thurmond had its own electric light plant by 1908, and entertained itself at the Thurmond Novelty Theater. It was a heady time.

It is unlikely that anyone foresaw it in 1910, but events soon to unfold would bring the downfall of Thurmond. Disaster did not come swiftly, for the town prospered during the 'teens and most of the '20's. This period began with the sale of the town to the Bullock Realty Company by Captain Thurmond's heirs. Thereafter, the "activities of the town were no longer the activities of the Thurmond family," as the Captain's grandson put it a half-century later, and perhaps the tone of the place relaxed a little as George Bullock settled in as mayor, landlord, notary and postmaster. The transfer does not seem to have had any effect on the town's fortunes, however. Thurmond continued as a major coal shipper and as a services and distribution hub for the coalfields. In 1922, for example, the Hudson Wholesale Fruit and Produce Company was receiving carload shipments several times a week and making its own daily deliveries to stores in the area. There was even some talk of relocating the county seat to the boom town by the river, at least until a newspaper observed that the courthouse "would have to hang from a cliff like a picture on the wall."

Nonetheless, changes were eroding Thurmond's position. Among the first important events was West Virginia state prohibition, effective in 1914. The town founder would have approved the ensuing drought, but nonetheless it cost the community one of its major attractions. "Prohibition cooled off the town," as State Archivist Kyle McCormick reflected in 1959, adding that "good roads and a bad name finished it." Thurmond got its own good road in 1917, twisting down Dunloup Creek from Glen Jean, but it was the roads built elsewhere in the area that hurt the riverside town. No longer was it necessary for regional distribution centers to be located on a mainline railroad, and the larger communities of Beckley and Oak Hill would soon predominate.

Nor was Thurmond's place in the regional rail network itself secure. The town's prosperity had always depended on its strategic importance in the Chesapeake & Ohio system, as a junction serving an important coal hinterland and as a repair and operations center. The completion of the Virginian Railway in 1909 opened competition to the C&O in Fayette

Above: **Train time was busy at Thurmond, even during mid-Depression. At this moment, the Mt. Hope local is just steaming onto the bridge on its way out of town, at right, and attention has shifted to the mainline train.** Photo by William Monypeny, August 1935; courtesy C&O Historical Society.

Below: **This panorama of southside Thurmond was shot from the other side of New River, directly across from the mouth of Dunloup Creek. The Dunglen Hotel dominates this view, with the Collins Cash Mercantile building to the right, across Dunloup. The Dunglen walkway crosses from the hotel to the road grade, at right. Residences and other smaller buildings surround the Collins building. The three-story building on the hill to the left of the hotel is the Masonic lodge, which had more members than Thurmond had citizens.** Photo by R. E. "Red" Ribble, between 1911 and 1922; from the collection of George Bragg.

County, and the 1910 connection of Bill McKell's Kanawha, Glen Jean & Eastern short-line railroad to the Virginian line at Pax tapped Thurmond's local mineral monopoly from the back side. No longer was the New River rail town the only outlet for Dunloup basin coal.

Thurmond's locational advantages also lessened with changes in the pattern of local mining. Gradually the coal industry shifted backwards from the gorge to New River tributaries, and eventually to the surrounding plateau itself. Thurmond, which had enjoyed a hammerlock on provisioning the industry so long as most of it lay along the C&O's riverside main line, became less important as a distribution center as the portion of the coalfield it served became relatively less important. This accelerated as the gorge was mined out and as Fayette County coal production as a whole declined in later years.

Thurmond suffered a damaging physical blow in late November 1922, with the great fire on the south side. Burned to the ground was a major business center, the frame building housing the dry goods and grocery operations of the Collins Cash Mercantile Company, as well as the Collins mortuary, the Lykens Drugstore, Stanley Panas' shoe shop, a movie theater and several second-floor apartments. State prohibition had closed the Ballyhack saloons, and now the core of respectable southside businesses was lost as well. Wallace Bennett, a resident at the time, dates the decline of the town from this fire. "Thurmond was never the same after that," he said in a 1980 interview.

Such conflagrations had played a major role in community history. But as in other boom towns, Thurmond's earliest fires had been in some ways beneficial, clearing initial and often flimsy construction for replacement. When Captain Thurmond's original frame hotel building burned in 1899, it was replaced by the solid brick Thurmond Hotel, and when the C&O depot burned in 1903, the railroad moved right away to erect a better structure. Fires became debilitating only as the town aged and its economic vigor waned. Now there was little reason to rebuild. The Collins building was not replaced nor was the Dunglen Hotel, the second of the local landmark structures to go. Smaller fires nibbled at the town's housing stock during the Depression and after, and there was little urgency to replace residences as population

The Webb family were among the citizens of Thurmond early in the century. Mr. Webb had come to town with his mother before 1910 and kept his own family there until 1935, according to son Carlton, at right here. Photographer unknown, October 1929; from the New River Gorge National River collection.

dwindled from 462 to 339 from 1930 to 1940 and by another 120 in the next decade.

Matters came to a head in the 1930's, Thurmond's great time of trouble. The fateful decade opened with the Dunglen fire of 1930, leaving a gap in the town's appearance and a hole in its pride. The National Bank of Thurmond failed in 1931, and Armour moved its wholesale meat business to Beckley the following year, reportedly taking a large loss in selling its Thurmond building. New River Banking & Trust Company left for Oak Hill in 1935. In 1938, the Chesapeake & Potomac Telephone district offices moved to Beckley. By comparison, Thurmond's loss of a quarter of its population during these ten years seems almost inconsequential. The real loss of the 1930's was in the businesses that had made Thurmond a regional hub, businesses now mostly gone to the larger towns of the plateau.

What was left to Thurmond was the railroad, and it was the railroad that kept the town alive during the next two decades. The Chesapeake & Ohio had built up a major investment in the riverside community, its facilities beginning on the north side upstream of the

Thurmond city line. At this point the single-track bridge from the south side angled into a bustling rail yard complex. Immediately at the foot of the bridge was a long warehouse-office building, no longer standing. Here freight foreman Stud Ramsey had kept several employees hopping during the busy 1920's, transferring mainline freight for transhipment on the branch lines and receiving outgoing shipments. "I've seen an express train come in there and there'd be a mountain of express," a resident of the time recalled. "It'd take them 40 minutes to unload it."

Back from the warehouse, but still on the river side of the mainline, sat the 1903-04 depot, a fine two-story example of classic railroad architecture. The 135-foot-long building housed the ticket agent's office, flanked by separate waiting rooms for white men and white women, with a single black waiting room and a baggage room farther down. The floor above included the signal tower, projecting out for a clear view of eastbound and westbound tracks, two large train master rooms, a dispatcher's room, a small conductor's room and two interconnecting supply rooms, with a big freight office topping the baggage room at the western end. This is the decaying depot which still greets rail visitors as well as those crossing over by car from the south side, serving now as Thurmond's Amtrak station.

Below the depot a whole world of railroading opened out between the town and the river. The rails fanned into train assembly and service yards, anchored on the eastern end by a barnlike roundhouse. This massive building– rectangular despite its name -- squats at the edge of the narrow Thurmond land bench, pierced from end to end by two tracks. The roundhouse was a repair shop and also unofficial headquarters for off-duty crews — "loafers' glory," in the disapproving words of one lady of the town. Engineers came by to make out trip tickets after their runs, check assignments on the call board, and rehash railroading with fellow train men. A variety of sheds and other service structures surrounded the roundhouse, with a makeshift bunkhouse nearby. A 100-foot locomotive turntable lay oposite the upper end of the roundhouse, removed in the 1930's. Thurmond's east corporate line falls just below the roundhouse, and the yards continue from

here almost to the west corporate line more than a half-mile downstream, gradually tapering back to two tracks. A handsome four-locomotive concrete coaling tower, built in 1922 by the Chicago firm of Fairbanks and Morse, still stands sentry over the Thurmond yards.

This complex gave the C&O a big stake in Thurmond and the company had no intention to abandon the town. As Charles Thurmond had anticipated a half-century before, Thurmond remained an important point on the line. It was a major stop for through trains on the C&O's Hinton Division, the only place between Handley and divisional headquarters at Hinton where locomotives might take on both coal and water. Thurmond was the train assembly and car distribution point for the local coalfield. The train crews "pulling and supplying" most Fayette County mines worked out of Thurmond, and Thurmond shops serviced the branchline locomotives which these men relied upon.

Thus, trains continued to rumble through Thurmond during the hardest times of the Great Depression. They now often carried a full complement of hoboes, and during the desperate spring of 1932 the Washington-bound "Bonus

Mrs. McClure's restaurant, with its flags and GI portraits, was a center of patriotic pride during World War II. Troops in uniform ate free. Photographer unknown, from the New River Gorge National River collection.

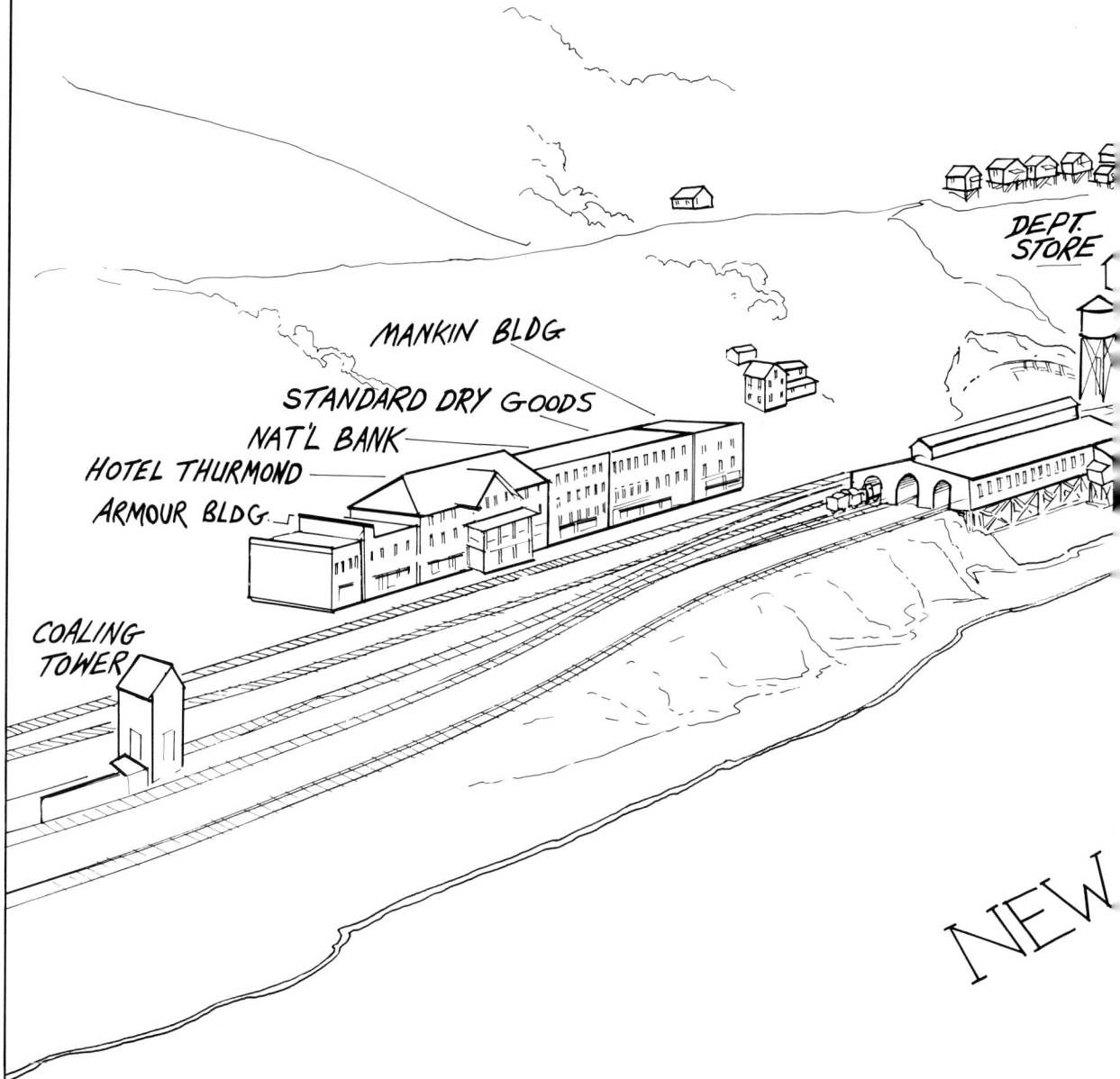

CONCEPTUAL SCHEMATIC
THURMOND, W.VA. CIRCA 1910-1920

DEPT. STORE

MANKIN BLDG
STANDARD DRY GOODS
NAT'L BANK
HOTEL THURMOND
ARMOUR BLDG

COALING TOWER

NEW

Andy Willis

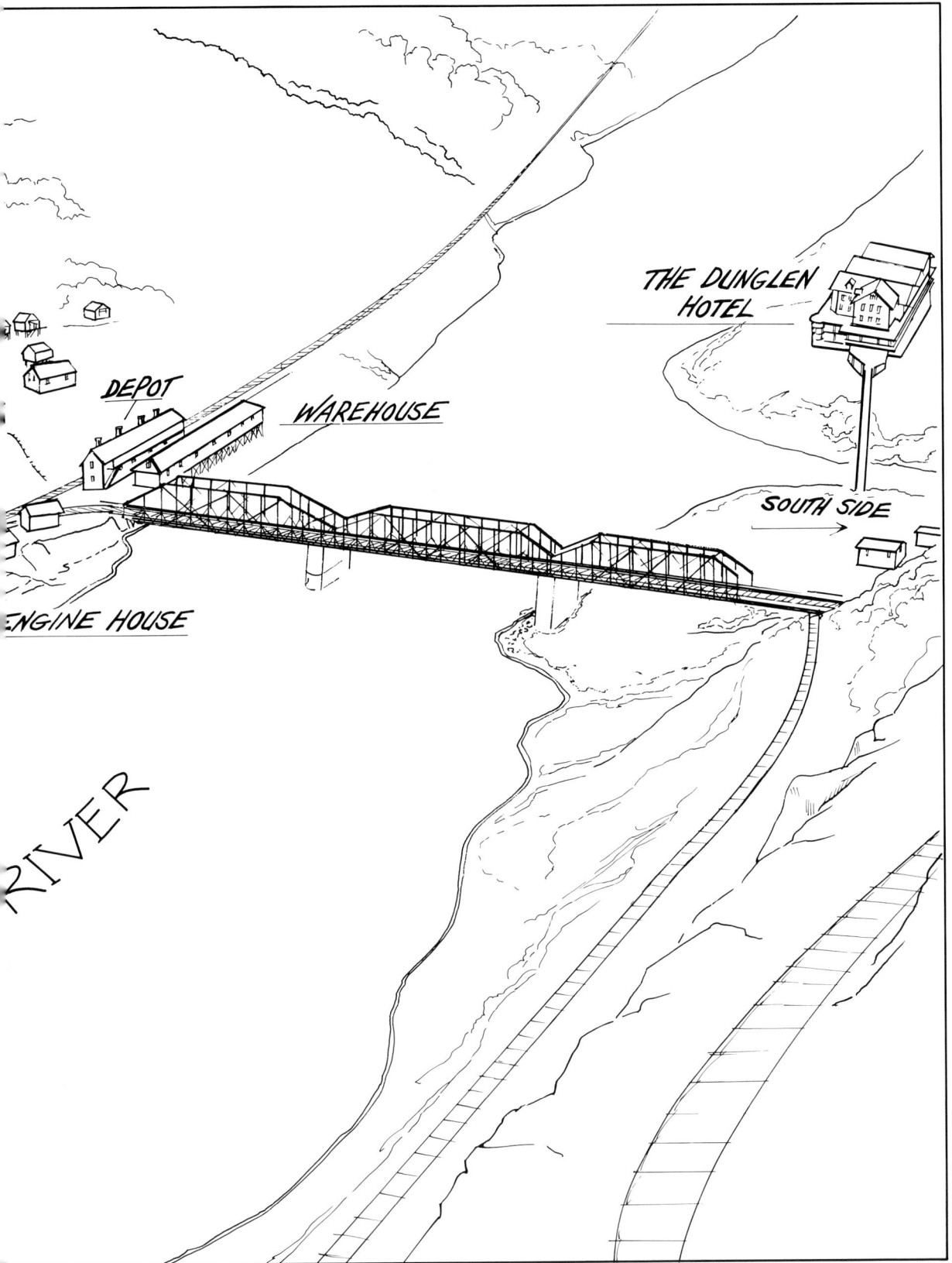

THE DUNGLEN
HOTEL

DEPOT

WAREHOUSE

SOUTH SIDE

ENGINE HOUSE

RIVER

The Thurmond yards in the late days of steam. Photographer unknown, 1946; courtesy C&O Historical Society.

Army" of jobless World War I veterans as well, but still they provided work for the generally more fortunate Thurmonders. Traffic picked up during the war that followed the Depression years, as women took over the switches in the train yard to rush men and military supplies through to the East Coast. Old Thurmonders still pride themselves on their town's war service, many pointing out that a GI in uniform could count on a free meal at Mrs. McClure's restaurant.

It was railroad dieselization that finally undid the riverside community, for Thurmond was a steam town, much of its economy built upon the crewing needs and short service intervals of steam locomotives. As a major coal carrier the Chesapeake & Ohio initially resisted the post-World War II rush to diesel motive power, seeking instead to develop steam turbines or coal-fired gas turbines. Competitive pressures from other railroads built up as the C&O's attempts to improve coal technology floundered, however. In 1949 the C&O purchased its own first diesel engines, still hoping that these new locomotives might serve only as

a stopgap until research put efficient coal burners on the rails. That day has not yet come, and during the 1950's Thurmonders watched helplessly as sleek diesels replaced the familiar steam engines in the C&O locomotive fleet. The change is still poignantly recalled. "No. 992 was the last steamer in Thurmond," according to former resident Dale Ernest, who upon a visit home in 1960 found the old engine parked on a sidetrack, "a cold, silent reminder."

Thurmond's story for the last half-century has been a story of steady decline. Population has dropped each decade, from a high of 462 people counted in the 1930 census to the 67 reported in 1980. The town that lost its business vitality in the Great Depression was hit a bare 20 years later by a devastating change in the technology of the railroad it served. Physical deterioration accelerated, with a final great fire in April 1963 gutting the old Armour building and the Lafayette Hotel, formerly the proud Hotel Thurmond. Today the 1922 coaling tower, built at Thurmond's proud peak but now home only to pigeons, joins these ruins of the business district as monuments to the town's twin misfortunes.

CHAPTER THREE

"Busy all the Time"

Community Life

Above all, Thurmond was a railroad town. "The railroad was life," as a 1919-35 resident observed, "our means of bread and butter." The community with no main street had a major trunk line railroad, one of America's great thoroughfares, running by its door. The passage of trains through town, the assembly of trains in the rail yards, the servicing of trains at the roundhouse, and the coming and going of passengers and the movement of freight at the station -- these were the things that governed life in Thurmond. The town went to work in the morning with the seven o'clock roundhouse whistle, paused for lunch with the noon whistle, and caught its breath with the C&O shift change at three.

The rumble of trains on tracks never ceased, nor did the activity of the men who served the trains and tracks. Railroaders worked their shifts--"tricks" in the parlance of the road-- alternately around the clock, and some part of Thurmond was always awake to attend to the C&O men. Hot meals or packed lunches might be had late at night in the hotels and restaurants, and rest taken in the afternoon at home or in the trackside bunkhouse. Thurmond took care of its railroaders and a C&O man knew he could count on the assistance of friends there. "I've always said if I had to be down and out, I'd rather have it happen to me in Thurmond than any place I knew of," said retired railroad telegrapher John Richmond. "Because in Thurmond I knew I'd get help."

Most of the town worked for the railroad in one way or another. The largest single group of wage earners within the corporate limits were direct Chesapeake & Ohio employees, accounting for more than 40% of the town's workforce in 1910. Train crews -- engineers, firemen, brakemen and conductors -- and machinists and other skilled shopmen, railroad agents, telegraphers and a variety of office workers were among those on the C&O payroll. Railroad jobs were considered the best in town and many a youngster aspired no higher. "My mother never talked to me about going to college or being an entrepreneur," recalls Thurmond native Carlton Webb, a man who learned to read by deciphering the lettering on boxcars. "She always told me to get a good job on the railroad."

Thurmonders not holding down any of those good jobs probably served the railroad indirectly, relying on the spent wages of C&O men for much of their own income. Store clerks sold railroaders the necessities and luxuries of life, bankers safeguarded their money, and barbers trimmed their hair. Other residents worked for businesses dependent upon rail transportation,

The movement of railroad rolling stock governed the pace of life in Thurmond. Here No. 1041 heads for the yards. Photo by Gene Huddleston, 1954; courtesy C&O Historical Society.

including wholesale distributors and the coal industry. There were few in Thurmond whom the C&O failed to touch.

Railroaders or not, most Thurmonders worked in the service occupations -- providing transportation, communications and wholesaling and retailing. Thurmonders poured beer, shipped meat, papered walls, and operated the telegraph and telephone. There was not a single manufacturing worker living within the town in 1910. A mere three men made their living by timbering, at a time when the West Virginia lumber industry was at its peak. Miners were equally rare in 1910, and apparently altogether absent in other years. "I used to know every human being, cat and dog down there, and I don't know of a single miner," Wallace Bennett recalls of his 1918-33 residency in the town. Thurmond made its money by sending New River coal to market, not by taking it from the ground.

That Thurmond produced no tangible product by all its hard labor set it apart from neighboring towns in the coalfields. The service nature of Thurmond's work had important internal implications, as well. In Thurmond, for example, women might work for pay. Most stayed home to raise families and fight the grime and coal dust of a trackside town, but many held regular jobs. A Thurmond woman might work as a clerk, office worker, waitress, milliner, teacher, domestic servant or telephone operator, among other occupations. Jacqueline Pugh grew up in Thurmond the daughter of a railroader, married and stayed on to keep store and eventually manage a landmark restaurant and hotel. She and her husband became leaders in the tourist trade of the new Thurmond. There were few such opportunities available for women in Fayette County coal towns of the period.

The railroad was always Thurmond's main boss, but men and women there worked for many other employers as well. Thurmond never became a company town, another fact setting it apart from most neighboring communities. Although Thurmond throughout its early history was largely owned by one family -- or two, to count the McKells and their holdings outside the city limits -- and was primarily a one-industry town all its life, the town owners and the dominant industry were not one and the same. The owners were not the principal employers

Above: **The Dog Wagon is remembered by many Thurmonders. The tiny food stand was diagonally across the tracks from the depot, handy to the traveling public.**
Photographer unknown, 1916; courtesy C&O Historical Society.

Below: **Thurmond benefited from entertainment traveling the C&O main line, including the popular "Silas Green from New Orleans" show. This 1925 view is of the south side, looking up Dunloup Creek. The original Collins Building has burned by this time and the store at right, once a saloon, houses the Collins enterprises as well as the South Side Shoe Repair Shop.**
Photographer unknown, from the New River Gorge National River collection.

The railroad was Thurmond's main employer, the source of the best jobs in town. This 1917 photograph shows C&O shop workers. Photographer unknown, from the New River Gorge National River collection.

and Thurmond was never simply a residential adjunct to an industrial operation. Nor was there any attempt to monopolize local business in the hands of the owners. Captain Thurmond cornered key elements of the local economy in building his bank and hotel, but anyone willing to pay him rent was free to go into any other line of trade. Outside the town proper but within the larger community, the McKells built another bank and hotel and allowed the variety of saloons prohibited inside corporate Thurmond as well as the many legitimate enterprises of the south side. Free of the economic repressiveness of employer-owned company towns

Black workers held the lower jobs at Thurmond's shops and yards. The men shown here were mostly classified as laborers and helpers on the C&O payroll. Excerpt from photo by R. E. "Red" Ribble, 1923; from the New River Gorge National River collection.

This February 1918 picture of the shop force includes an unidentified woman, possibly a clerical worker. The popular machininst, D. H. "Dad" Nugent, stands at right. Photographer unknown, from the New River Gorge National River collection.

and spurred by the business and personal competitiveness of two coalfield dynasties, Thurmond in its prime developed a dynamic, varied economy.

Thurmond also differed from the surrounding coal towns in its residential patterns. The town's original housing core consisted of the 30 or more rental dwellings built by Captain Thurmond. To these were added other residences outside the city limits, on both sides of the river. Thurmond's locally most distinguishing housing feature was its apartments. Families lived over the businesses of the main commercial block, upstairs in the Collins Building on the south side, and wherever else modest quarters might be fitted in. Building and living space always remained "scarce and expensive" in Thurmond, as 1927-32 resident Herman Monk remembered. Mr. Monk himself rented an apartment in the Armour Building, his place of employment. For $15 monthly he enjoyed five or six rooms, "enough that I could subrent some of it and get my rent free thataway."

Single men and married men living away from home were apt to board with families or room in a boarding house or hotel. If these men were black, they might "batch" in trackside shanty cars. These converted railroad cars were lined up along lower Dunloup Creek, on the south side. The shanty cars represented the worst of the community's housing, with the houses and apartments within Thurmond proper generally considered the best. Areas outside the city limits, consisting mainly of McKell rental properties, were less desirable. Services were poorer outside corporate Thurmond, with Bill McKell accused of piping unpurified river water to his houses on the north side's east end.

Blacks and immigrants contributed mightily to the industrialization of southern West Virginia, but relatively few made it into the service economy of Thurmond. The community was composed mostly of native white citizens, with those living inside the city limits almost entirely so. There were fewer than a half-dozen independent black families in Thurmond proper in 1910. The few single blacks were mostly attached to white households, including three servants working at the Thurmond Hotel and one at the Hubbard boarding house. Blacks were more numerous on the south side and fairly common in the local work force.

Except for the few engaged in domestic service, most worked as laborers or helpers at the roundhouse, in the rail yards, or on railroad

From Thurmond's lower end, the westbound tracks swept around the bend and off toward Cincinnati. This area included some of the town's best housing, both at track level and on the hillside above. Photographer and date unknown, from the New River Gorge National River collection.

section gangs. Thurmond was not an equal opportunity employer.

Immigrants were scarcer even than blacks. There were five living in Thurmond proper in 1910, all from Great Britain. Undoubtedly, there were a few more outside the city limits and thus not tallied with Thurmond in the census. Immigrants did not face the level of discrimination suffered by blacks. Glen Jean Mayor Leo Schaffer, one of the area's best-known residents, was foreign born, and other immigrants occupied prominent positions. Mr. and Mrs. Thomas Scott, in charge at the Thurmond Hotel, were both of Scottish birth. Across the river at the Dunglen a reputedly overbearing German headwaiter held sway at about the same time, once narrowly surviving a shooting fracas with the hotel's black cook. That the aggrieved black man was the one to leave town in a hurry spoke much of the relative standing of blacks and immigrants in the community.

Standing astride the C&O main line, Thurmond had no trouble keeping in touch with America. Big city newspapers arrived at the depot newsstand or by subscription on Thurmond's doorsteps on the date of publication. The riverside town also enthusiastically took to radio when that exciting new medium appeared. American broadcasting was less than two years old when in August 1922 the Fayette Tribune reported that town landlord George Bullock had a General Electric radio while another citizen was "assembling one of his own creation." Within a few years Doc Ridge had become a radio dealer, and those who had not yet bought a set of their own gathered at his South Side Drug Company -- so called even after moving to the north side -- to listen for free. As radios became more common, Thurmonders tuned in the popular programs of the day, including "Amos 'n' Andy" and the Lowell Thomas newscasts.

From time to time, newsmakers graced the town with their presence. The "Great Commoner," populist William Jennings Bryan, made a whistle-stop speech from the back of a train during his 1908 Democratic presidential campaign. Bryan packed the town, according to one

At
1947
Success

people, repre-

Mrs. McClure's restaurant remained a popular gathering place in postwar Thurmond. Mrs. McClure rests her elbow on the candy case in this scene from early 1948, with husband J. W. McClure beside her. Brakeman Jack Crow and Virginia Scott are the customers. Photographer unknown, courtesy Wallace Bennett.

who was there, even though Republican William Howard Taft later carried Fayette County by a wide margin. Evangelist Billy Sunday drew a crowd upon a later visit. Sunday preached at the Dunglen and collected the cash offering in dishpans. "He made an announcement not to let the pan rattle," a witness recently recalled. "He wanted greenbacks instead of change."

Other traveling preachers passed through from time to time, but Thurmond ordinarily preferred homegrown religion. The town supported two mainstream churches during its heyday, with both Methodist and Baptist congregations present for several years after 1906. Black worshipers met less formally on the south side, so at times there were several groups active at once. Throughout most of its history, however, Thurmond has found siritual solace at a single house of worship, the white clapboard church that stands high on the hillside east of the corporate line. Burned and rebuilt on the same site, this church was first organized under Baptist auspices but has been a nondenominational "union" congregation in recent times.

The youngsters of Thurmond attended school according to their race. The school for black children hung precariously on the hillside below the upper street, west of the clapboard church but still outside the city limits. Heating coal was lowered down by a washtub and cable, while students and teacher clambered in under their own power. White children were better served, first by a one-room school and then by a two-room structure which itself was later expanded. Thurmond's reputation scared away hardy young male teachers during the rowdier years, a future state attorney general among them, but the white school seems to have been ably served by young women during most times. Miss Annie Huddleston, the town's first teacher, set the pattern for those who followed. Scholars wishing to advance beyond grade school attended high school on the plateau, taking the local passenger train up to Mt. Hope after the building of the Glen Jean branch railroad.

29

Nobody called Thurmond a garden spot, but the C&O kept flowers and a fountain by its "safety first" sign, near the roundhouse. Excerpt from photo by R. E. "Red" Ribble, 1928; from the New River Gorge National River collection.

Entertainment was of both the homemade and imported varieties. Traveling shows made regular stops, with the big "Silas Green from New Orleans" black minstrel show among the most recalled today. Thurmond's ballplayers took over the carnival grounds in the creek bottom near the Dunglen on many summer weekends. A former resident remembers easy victories over teams form nearby Weewin and Beury Mountain, but trouble elsewhere. "When we'd come up Loup Creek to play Red Star or Glen Jean, they'd beat the tar clean out of us," Wallace Bennett recalls.

There were more genteel activities for the women of the town. Some busied themselves in church work, while others preferred an active club life. Former postmistress Jane Lawson recalls a ladies' aid society and a garden club, among other diversions. "There was always something," she says. "There were so many clubs and so many things going on that you really were busy all the time." When necessary, Thurmond women rallied for more serious

tasks, sometimes working all night to feed train wreck victims, for example.

Men enjoyed an even livelier social life as Thurmond became a coalfields lodge center. In 1920, with the census reporting 285 people within the city limits, Thurmond had a fraternal lodge population of 871. The Knights of Pythias, Moose and Royal Arch Masons were all present, with the latter, at 601 members, by far the most popular. The Masons had moved their Beury chapter to southside Thurmond about 1911, building a new lodge hall soon afterwards. Thurmond chapters of the railway brotherhoods -- labor unions with social and fraternal features -- claimed an additional 311 members, for a total local membership of nearly 1200. Men might find more vigorous diversion in the saloons and dives of Ballyhack or -- after prohibition -- courtesy of Thurmond's bootleggers.

The population on both sides of the river never approached 1200 males eligible to join a lodge, and even allowing for multiple membership this figure suggests that Thurmond was supplying recreation to much of the surrounding area. That such regional recreation was another important service of the riverside town is supported by the memory of past residents. For New River mining people seeking escape from drab coal town, Thurmond was a close as a short train ride on payday. They transformed the town when they came. "The sidewalk looked like Broadway there on Saturday night," Herman Monk recalls of the miners who swarmed in. "They'd bring their wives and children, too, you know. They had stayed on the job a whole week and that gave them some bright lights on Saturday night." Mr. Monk remembers the No. 8 passenger train being so crowded on these occasions that it had to stop between stations to allow the conductor time to collect tickets.

Many Thurmonders found wholesome family recreation in gardening along the riverbank, on hillside terraces or other available scraps of land. Residents gathered berries in the mountains and fished in the river. Townspeople of both sexes and all ages swam in New River, the wiser ones with a healthy respect for the unpredictable current. Thurmond children did about what their contemporaries elsewhere did. "We all played ball, shot marbles and swam a lot," recalls a boy of 1930's Thurmond, adding that – unknown to the C&O -- idle railway locomotives provided giant educational toys to many future trainmen.

In short, Thurmonders worked and played, went to church on Sunday and perhaps partied some the night before, raised families and planned for the future. There was nothing very exceptional in this. In the rich variety of its life Thurmond differed from neighboring company towns, stunted in their own development by a narrow economic mission, but these coal towns diverged more sharply from the norm than did the railroad town by the river. For most of its history Thurmond itself was not greatly different from other American working class towns of comparable size and circumstances. The town was as normal as its citizens could make it, with their steady work habits and their lodges and clubs and ladies' aid societies. Thurmond had its rowdy side, and a wilder adolesence than most places, but within

Despite its rough-and-ready reputation, most former residents today recall Thurmond as a peaceful town and a good place to grow up. Here paperboy Carlton Webb pauses for a moment with Mr. Oliver, in front of Mrs. McMillan's boarding house. Photographer unknown, August 1932; from the New River Gorge National River collection.

the city limits generations of people lived and died in relative peace and comfort.

A longtime Thurmonder may have had such thoughts in mind when she described her community in words that would fit many another small town. "Everybody knew everybody else's business," she commented. "Everybody knew when anyone was sick or they needed help. And when they needed help, they took up money and helped them. It was just that type of place to live."

31

The Dunglen Hotel sat upstream and across the river from Thurmond proper. This photograph appears to have been made soon after construction was completed in 1901. Photo by William O. Trevey, from the collection of Bill Hickman.

The Dunglen Hotel

A popular Thurmond story tells of the time coal operator Paddy Rend sold his Arbuckle Creek mine to industrial magnate Edward J. Berwind for better than a million dollars. Rend is supposed to have shown the check around the bar, bought drinks for all and then stepped aboard the outbound train to be seen no more. The year was 1904 and the place could have been nowhere but the Dunglen Hotel. The Dunglen was Fayette County's finest, the place where the big deals were done and the good liquor drunk, and it is the one place at Thurmond most remembered today.

The life of the Dunglen was short, the 29 years from its construction in 1901 to destruction by fire in 1930. Fortunately for the hotel's reputation, those years happened to be the right ones, encompassing the boom times of Thurmond's history. Thurmond was at its best during those three decades, and by all accounts the best of Thurmond was the big hotel on the south side.

The Dunglen was a rambling, three-and-a-half-story building, surrounded by a double-decker porch on three of its sides and with its name proudly proclaimed in giant letters on the roof. The architecture was an eclectic wood-frame style common to the turn of the century. Its location across the river by the mouth of Dunloup Creek put it away from the worst din of the tracks and rail yards of the north side. This was a considerable advantage over the competing Hotel Thurmond, from whose porch it was said a good marksman could spit tobacco juice onto passing trains. Still, the Dunglen was conveniently connected by the New River bridge and its own pedestrian bridge over Dunloup. Porters ferried back and forth, claiming passengers at the northside depot and carting their baggage back to the hotel. Two dollars and a half would buy one of the hotel's 100 rooms during the early years, although the Dunglen's better accommodations went for $4 per night.

As the best hotel in the area, the Dunglen quickly established itself as the business and social hub of the New River Coalfield. The hotel was where mine investors stayed while they inspected their local holdings, and where deals such as Rend's were celebrated. Visiting preachers found a podium at the Dunglen and visiting gamblers a warm seat, and like the coal financiers they both carried cash out of the town. That all got along together suggests that, despite the frolicsome reputation the Dunglen has since acquired, it was not as notorious at the time as the surrounding establishments of the Ballyhack district. The hotel bar was not mentioned in *The Whiskey Ring*, the scandalous pamphlet that scoured Dunloup from mouth to headwaters to report the worst joints for political advantage in the 1912 election. "Even here, one took one's chances," however, as a frequent Dunglen visitor later recalled.

Society dances were held at the Dunglen, and faithfully reported in the local press. The hotel management sought further such business with the addition of a new dance hall in 1921, opened with a big dance in November. The new Dunloup Creek automobile road was bringing local celebrants in increasing numbers by this time, and manager H. T. Lyttleton announced that he wished to make a "sort of social center" of his hotel. It was a political center as well, hosting gatherings distinctly less genteel than ballroom dances. Judge Meredith Sims reportedly called one political meeting to order by pounding his Colt .45, then used the six-shooter as a handy gavel throughout the debate.

The Dunglen was built by the landowning McKells but never actively managed by them. Rather, it went through a series of managers, leasors and owners. Quality varied with the management, as with any other hostelry. Butterfield, the high-toned first

THE DUNGLEN

THE DUNGLEN HOTEL COMPANY, Proprietors.

H. M. Personette, Manager.   THURMOND, W. VA.

Rate, $2.50 to $4.00.

THE LEADING HOTEL IN THIS SECTION.

There was no doubt that the Dunglen was "the leading hotel in this section," as this 1906 advertisement claims. From the *Official Industrial Guide and Shippers Directory*, C&O Railway.

manager, was soon respected as a leader of the community -- a position confirmed when his daughter entered the local gentry by marrying the prominent industrialist and politician, as well as physician, Dr. Gory Hogg. Other managers were less respected and less effectve. Local coal operator George Wolfe recalled one, a Mr. Post, as "about the worst hotel manager I have ever run across." Things got so bad under Post's stewardship that the big hotel ended up with no lights and no heat on at least one cold winter night, Wolfe remembered.

The Dunglen was the place traveling wholesalers showed their wares to local merchants, and it housed several permanent businesses as well. A mortuary, grocery, dry goods store, drugstore, shoe shop, furniture store and theater are among the Dunglen commercial tenants remembered today. The presence of these operations on the Dunglen's lower level made the hotel southside Thurmond's commercial center, especially after a 1922 fire destroyed the Collins Building.

Like much else about Thurmond, the grandeur of the Dunglen has been embroidered over the years. The hotel was fine "for those days," as Raleigh County coal operator W. P. Tams later reported, and no doubt the best on the Chesapeake & Ohio between Charleston and Hinton. However, it seems unlikely that it ever seriously competed for leisure business with major Eastern resorts, as is often said. The wealth of the Dunglen was the raw wealth of a booming coalfield, and the hotel caught the attention of the nation's rich and powerful only when their affairs brought them to New River.

By any measure, the Dunglen Hotel was an important part of Thurmond, its spirit if not its heart, and a major element of the local economy. Its loss to fire in 1930, amid charges and countercharges of arson, was a grievous one. The fire "killed this side of the river," a contemporary recalled of the Thurmond south side, and it is safe to say it didn't do the rest of the town any good, either.

The merchants of Thurmond's main commercial block attracted respectable business to the town, while saloons of the south side, across the river and legally in Glen Jean, built a bad reputation for the community. Photographer and date unknown, from the New River Gorge National River collection.

CHAPTER FOUR

Hell With a River Through It
The Legend

"You have heard of the California gold rush
Way back in forty-nine,
But Thurmond, on New River,
Will beat it every time.
There's people here from everywhere,
The colored and the white,
Some mother's son bites the dust
Almost every night."

The verse is by a railroad man, Captain H. W. Doolittle, a C&O conductor who knew Thurmond well. His 1902 poem spoke of another side of the New River town, the boisterous side not condoned by Captain Thurmond and the respectable people who lived within his corporate limits. Ironically, the town that Captain Doolittle glorified is the town most recalled today.

Doolittle's Thurmond was the Thurmond of popular legend, wild and glamorous. It had a fancy resort hotel for those who could afford it, and an array of saloons, dance halls and houses of ill repute for the rest. The town depot handled tens of thousands of people annually-- more than 75,000 in 1910 -- and it is not to be supposed that all of them came to Thurmond on respectable business. Nor may we assume that they all got along in perfect harmony once there, for above all the Thurmond of legend was a dangerous place. "A man didn't dare walk along the railroad tracks after dark with a lighted lantern or a cigarette in his mouth," bartender "Speck" Davis later recalled. "Somebody would be sure to shoot out the light."

Thurmond enthusiast Eugene Scott, after interviewing Davis and his contemporaries from the boom period, concurred. "In Thurmond, at the turn of the century, killings were almost an everyday occurrence."

In respect for Captain Thurmond's good name, it must be noted that the Thurmond of legend was not really Thurmond at all, but rather the adjacent area actually within extended Glen Jean. One passed from one municipality to the other by crossing the river, or merely by stepping across the corporate line at the upper end of Dr. Mankin's red brick building, but by any other measure the distance was great. The town of Glen Jean was ruled over by men less given to enforcing the proprieties than was stern W. D. Thurmond. In fact, they seemed often to partake of impropriety themselves. The result was a wide-open community, with permissiveness seeping from the top down.

Mayor Leo Schaffer was the highest local authority, alternately presiding at riverside and in upper Glen Jean. Schaffer was a colorful figure, an immigrant businessman who first settled downstream at Sewell around 1888. By the 1890's he had moved to southside Thurmond. As a Jew of Austrian birth Schaffer was unlike his neighbors, but nonetheless became the popular mayor of Glen Jean. If the stories are accurate, he sometimes took a participatory approach to the problem of crime, sampling the fruit of the evils he was sworn to correct.

Everyone's favorite Schaffer story, and perhaps the most famous Thurmond tale of all, is of the mayor's summary handling of a death inquest. It seems that the body of an armed man had been discovered, a not uncommon event in the legendary riverside town. Schaffer did his investigating on the spot, fining the dead man the contents of his wallet for carrying a gun and then confiscating the offending pistol as evidence. Thus impoverished, the victim was handed over for burial at the expense of Fayette County taxpayers. The story varies with the teller, but the usual implication is that the spoils pocketed by the mayor never made it into the coffers of the town of Glen Jean.

Virginia Mankin lived in Thurmond during these years, and she told a more elaborate version of the tale as solemn truth. "A drunk Italian had two visitors from Pittsburgh come to see him. He said he would teach them to fly. He mounted a big rock just above the bridge and jumped into the river. The strong undercurrent washed him up at Rush Run," the doctor's wife related in an interview some years later. When the body was found Mayor Schaffer was duly called upon, and supposedly fined the victim the $81 he carried, plus his gold watch, "for committing suicide in the corporate limits." Mrs. Mankin's son helped carry the body and witnessed the whole proceedings, she reported. "An undertaker came from Pittsburgh to remove the remains back home. Harrison Ash beat him up and threw him in the lock-up," she concluded. Mrs. Mankin agreed that the corpse was finally buried at county expense, specifically recalling the fee as $10.

Ash, Leo Schaffer's contemporary at Thurmond, left the reputation of a lawman of easy conscience. He was hired as marshal around 1902, at about age 48, having served as a railroad detective since leaving his native Tennessee. Ash carried a notched pistol, with estimates of the number of his official killings varying from seven to 18. At six-foot-four and 275 pounds, he made a lasting impression on young Howard B. Lee, later West Virginia's attorney general. "After supper as I sat in the hotel lobby watching the milling crowd, in walked a giant of a man," Lee recalled of an overnight visit to the Dunglen in 1905. "He wore a gaudy uniform, with the word 'CHIEF' on his broad brimmed Stetson hat."

A newspaper of the day described the bearded Ash as a "stalwart specimen of mankind," lauding his accomplishments, but a later journalist probably came closer to the truth in saying he "was able to keep order largely by terrorizing the lawless." Order within his own family evidently eluded the marshal, however, for when Mrs. Ash stood trial for murder in 1910 it emerged that she had accidentally shot the wrong party while gunning for her husband. By that year Ash had fallen off a cliff, injuring his leg and subsequently undergoing surgery in Huntington, and finally settled down as a truck farmer across the county in Deep Water. He would trouble Thurmond bad men no more.

With men like Ash and Schaffer in charge, it is not surprising that instability prevailed in the Thurmond of legend. Sometimes the general lawlessness was turned against the town fathers themselves. A couple of celebrants broke out of Ash's jail on one occasion and took their grievances out on the Glen Jean mayor. They "caught Leo Schaffer and held him up by a foot each and dangled him over New River from the center of the bridge," according to Mrs. Mankin. She got this account from Dr. Mankin, who happened by on his mule in time to extract a promise that His Honor would not be dropped into the rushing water. Ash likewise emerged less than triumphant at times, reportedly being faced down by a black fugitive on Dunloup Creek one dark night, for example.

Mankin, Lee and the versifying Captain Doolittle were all respectable eyewitnesses, and no doubt there is truth in the stories they told. The whole truth of Thurmond added up to something less than the sum of such parts, however, for the community was not as wild and lawless as the individual stories suggest. Contrary to Doolittle's poem, no mother's son died there "almost every night," nor even every week or every month. In fact, in 1902, the year he penned "Thurmond on New River," only some mother's daughter died of violence in the riverside town, according to Fayette County death records. Martha Ellis, a 19-year-old single white woman, died of a gunshot wound on December 10. The other two deaths recorded at Thurmond that year were of peaceful, natural causes. It is possible that some homicides went

36

Broken windows and robust customers were about par for the saloons of Thurmond's Ballyhack district. Here (left to right) Al and George Treadway and John and Jeff Johnson line up outside the South Side Saloon, while Henry Brown takes refuge behind a post.   Photographer unknown, about 1910; from the New River Gorge National River collection.

unrecorded, and that Thurmond contributed some of the six gunshot fatalities listed upriver at McKendree Hospital that year. However, there is no evidence that Thurmond was a place of random, wanton bloodshed at the turn of the century.

Still, the place had its dangers. Nonfatal combat would not have produced statistics for the death records, and likely much of it was never reported to the authorities at all. Brawling was predictable in a community comprised disproportionately of men of the most volatile ages, especially where law enforcement was complicated by a split jurisdiction. There was also the constant danger of the railroad tracks, with trains barreling through the congested town day and night and grinding ceaselessly back and forth in the rail yards. The swift New River took its toll, too, offering nearby recreation and occasionally claiming an unfortunate swimmer in exchange. A single tragic drowning in the summer of 1919 carried away J. L. Howland and Mrs. Ora Keys, both residents of the

town. "They weren't all murdered," former Thurmond railroad agent F. J. Ginn declared, citing 11 deaths he knew of. "Some just fell in the river and drowned, some were found dead on the railroad tracks," although the agent recalled most as shootings.

Thus gunfire, steel rails and a merciless river each contributed their dangers to the uncertainties of life in Thurmond. Whether the town was significantly more hazardous than the surrounding region is open to question, however. Fayette County was a dangerous, violent place during its industrial boom. A single issue of the *Fayette Tribune*, December 28, 1911, reported that an immigrant woman had accidentally shot a neighbor on Christmas morning, murder had been committed in a Page saloon the same day, and a C&O engineer had died in a train wreck at McKendree. Milder excitement included a boy robbed of his father's pay at Stuart, a recent Clifftop company store robbery, and charges of gun theft, assault, bastardy and pistol-packing. A report of highwaymen around

Montgomery rounded out the front-page mayhem. Thurmond itself evidently remained quiet during the sacred holidays, as far as the *Tribune* editor knew.

If Thurmond was not exceptionally more violent than the neighboring area, how did it come to acquire its bad name? First, of course, there was fire enough behind the smoke of Thurmond's reputation. The popular characterization had sufficient basis in fact to capture the spirit of the place. The town averaged from one to two reported homicides per year at the turn of the century -- one each in 1900, 1901 and 1902, with three more for the three-year period at nearby locations which may actually have been southside Thurmond. This record does not substantiate the free-fire zone of popular legend, but it was killing enough for a community of not more than a few hundred residents. There were few times during the boom years when at least one murder was not fresh in the memory of Thurmonders.

There was also a glamor to Thurmond, compared to its drab neighbors, that no doubt contributed to the rail town's reputation. Thurmond was a pulsating, colorful place during its heyday, crackling with human and natural energy within the tight confines of the canyon walls. The earth shook as trains rumbled through and the mighty New River rushed by, the black diamond rolled out and hundreds of people embarked and disembarked daily. The smell of money hung tantalizingly in the air, and to that potent element was added the tang of adventure as night settled in the gorge and electric lights sparkled on along the veranda of the Dunglen and at a dozen lesser places of amusement. Clearly, Thurmond was the kind of place where extraordinary things might be expected to happen.

Such a scene was readymade for Thurmond's romanticizers and the town's current reputation is largely their doing. H. W. Doolittle's 1902 poem is the oldest recorded component of the legend, penned barely 15 years after earliest development of the town. Over the succeeding boom years, all the elements of the "biggest little town" argument fell into place and that label began appearing regularly in the state press. The sobriquet was used at least as early as 1914, in a *Pocahontas Independent* article

contrasting Thurmond's phenomenal coal tonnage and freight revenue to its small population. A lengthy article under the "Biggest Little Town" title appeared in the *Fayette Tribune* in 1920, taking the same tack while also pointing out that important people were taking note of the town by the river. The town precinct was voting two-to-one Democratic at the time, for example, with only 150-odd voters altogether, but West Virginia Republican official J. V. Sullivan was nonetheless impressed enough to characterize Thurmond as "one of the remarkable towns of the state."

Nobody would have agreed more than newspaperman Eugene Scott, Thurmond's greatest publicist. Born in Raleigh County in 1912, Scott never knew his favorite town during its prime years. He became editor of the *Beckley Post-Herald* in 1941, evidently first taking an interest in Thurmond a few years before that. Scott wrote of the river town in his newspaper and in 1946 produced an influential four-part series for the *West Virginia Review*, later reworked as a popular pamphlet. The introduction to the pamphlet spoke of the "days when champagne flowed like water at the Dunglen Hotel and hardly a night passed that murder was not done by the railroad bridge." All considered, the enthusiastic journalist concluded, Thurmond "during its heyday, was a town without parallel in the whole world." Both the pamphlet and magazine series included all the glamorous and violent aspects of the Thurmond legend, the series also preserving extensive interview excerpts from people present during Thurmond's boom.

The legend had taken on a life of its own by the time Scott made his rounds, and old Thurmonders were not hesitant to fill the ears of the young newspaperman. George Wolfe, formerly a Glen Jean mine superintendent, described his own 1901 arrival in detail. He had first come to Thurmond late at night, the coal man recalled, seeking refuge in the train station when warned that "someone might knock me in the head and throw me in the river." Next morning he found no personal danger but plentiful local color while taking breakfast at a boarding house. A traveling salesman carried his overcooked steak out to tenderize it with a rock on the railroad track,

Thurmond bustled in its heyday, as people flocked in from the surrounding coalfields in search of a good time. "The sidewalk looked like Broadway there on Saturday night," Herman Monk recalls.
Postcard view, about 1915; courtesy C&O Historical Society.

whereupon the landlady "grabbed up a butcher knife and took after the drummer, saying his actions were casting disgrace on her house."

Thurmond's legend was likewise promoted enthusiastically by the late Reverend Shirley Donnelly, Fayette County's popular amateur historian. The Oak Hill preacher is credited with coining one of the best-known character-izations of the town, fulminating at one point that "the only difference between Thurmond and hell is that a river runs through Thur-mond." The town's reputation has more recent-ly been embellished in a book and seminar paper by old Captain Thurmond's great-grand-son, Walter R. T. Witschey. A rare published attempt to deflate the legend was authored by Walter R. Thurmond in 1961, representing Thur-mond family chagrin of a generation earlier.

It may be significant that Thurmond boomed soon after the closing of the American frontier. The contemporary mythification of the West offered widely recognized imagery, available to Thurmond's colorful figures and to armchair romanticizers alike. Police Chief Ash conscious-ly modeled himself after dashing, "shoot-

first" western lawmen, with his Stetson and notched gun, and the unknown namer of the Black Hawk Saloon surely had some western antecedent in mind. Eugene Scott subtitled his pamphlet "Dodge City of West Virginia," and quoted Mrs. Mankin to the effect that there was "no Sunday west of Clifton Forge and no God west of Hinton," a slogan only slightly modi-fied from its origins in the Texas of Judge Roy Bean's time.

Whatever the truth of Thurmond's youth, there is no doubt that the town settled down with age. The saloons closed with state pro-hibition in 1914, less money circulated as the local economy stagnated, and there were fewer people jostling each other on Thurmond's side-walks. Residents of the late 1920's and after-wards recall the town as a quiet and peaceful place to live. Some resent the earlier repu-tation.

"I don't like to hear them call it Dodge City, because it wasn't like that," former postmis-tress Jane Graham Lawson says of her 1934-63 residency in the town. "It wasn't like that at all."

Thurmond is in its twilight as an industrial town now, the historic rail yards mostly silent.
Photo by Doug Chadwick.

EPILOGUE
Thurmond Reborn

Thurmond still lives, as its citizens will be quick to tell you. In the mid-1980's those citizens included people like retired locomotive engineer Jack Kelly, former town constable, town sergeant, fire warden air raid warden and tax collector, who had been there since 1917. Mr. Kelly lived high on the northside mountain near the Union Church, and for many years cultivated an elaborate system of terraced gardens adjacent to his house. He had found Thurmond a rewarding place to live most of a long life, and a town that keeps the loyalty of people like Jack Kelly has never quite died.

Still, you would not be very wrong in surmising that Thurmond has come close. The central business block is mostly gone or in ruins now. Thurmond remains an incorporated town, but the population at the 1980 census was barely a fifth of the number reported at the town's first official enumeration back in 1910. The C&O roundhouse and depot, once-proud symbols of a century of railroading, are falling into disrepair. The trainmen's bunkhouse is entirely gone, as are the turntable, the long riverside freight depot and many smaller structures. The big frame store building above the northside water tanks, once occupied by Hurvitz and Lopinsky's Leader general merchandise store and later by the Collins enterprises, has disappeared. Major landmarks of the south side -- the Dunglen Hotel, the original Collins building, and the saloons -- are likewise gone. Dwellings are scattered about, particularly on the north side, but physically you won't find much of the old Thurmond left.

What you will find is people -- and, depending on when you go, lots of people. These people hold Thurmond's hopes for an economic rebirth. They come today for the same reason many flocked to Thurmond in the past, to enjoy themselves. The attraction is no longer saloons, nightlife and a resort hotel, but primarily the New River. Thurmond's modern visitors are mostly whitewater rafters. They seek a wholesome day in the outdoors, although it is doubtful that the most gleeful hellraisers of 75 years ago had a livelier time than may be found in the rapids downstream when the big river is running full.

Wildwater Unlimited, the pioneering New River rafting outfitter, is headquartered at southside Thurmond, its base camp taking up part of the old Dunglen foundation. Most other local rafting companies also "put in" at or near Thurmond, bringing the total of people embarking daily in peak season to more than 2,000 by the mid-1980's. That is a good many more travelers than ever took a train out of Thurmond on any single day in the town's earlier history.

Commercial rafting on New River is a young industry, but the use of the river for recreation is as old as people's occupation of the gorge. Old Thurmonders recall fishing and swimming as major pastimes. Boating was popular in many parts of the gorge, although apparently not in the immediate Thurmond area. Deliberately running the rapids for fun seems not to have been done in earlier times, however, and the notion leaves many gorge natives incredulous today. New River rafting evidently made its appearance with a World War II army camp at Prince, which trained recruits in bridge building and sometimes ran rafting exercises downstream to Thurmond. Commercial rafting began with the founding of Wildwater Unlimited in 1968.

Thurmond's colorful past furnishes part of

the running commentary of rafting guides, and many of their guests spend some time viewing the town's ruins and remaining structures and musing over its history. Other visitors come for the history itself, including legions of railroad buffs over the years. The National Park Service recognizes the historical significance of the old rail town in planning for the surrounding New River Gorge National River, and is expected to boost Thurmond as a historical as well as recreational resource.

The historical attractiveness of Thurmond was underscored in a practical, dollars-and-cents way when a movie crew brought a multimillion-dollar budget to the riverside town in 1986. Producers of "Matewan" sought an early-1900's industrial setting for their story of a labor-management shootout in another West Virginia town. With some temporary alterations, Thurmond was found to fit the bill. Gun shots again rang out on the banks of New River, although there was no question of bloodshed this time.

The birth of the rafting industry and the establishment of the New River Gorge National River are major events in the recent history of the New River Gorge. These events are important to Thurmond, and Thurmond to them. The town, on the road in from National River headquarters at Glen Jean, remains one of the few gateways to the gorge. Thurmond's strategic location works to its economic advantage as public and private investment in New River tourism continues.

Thus, geography is still Thurmond's trump card, as recreational development of this part of the New River Gorge funnels through the historic town. The newfound wealth is more modest than that of the boom times, so far at least, and it comes today in the form of tourist dollars rather than the dirty black gold of rattling coal gondolas. But it finds its way down Dunloup Creek to Thurmond for the same reason as before: Practically speaking, there is no other way into this part of the gorge. Captain William Dabney Thurmond, who sized up the site's prospects more than a century ago, understood that very well.

Present-day visitors to Thurmond enjoy rafting and kayaking on the New River, which is rated among the premier whitewater rivers in America. National Park Service photo.

INDEX

BIBLIOGRAPHY

Anonymous, *The Whiskey Ring*. N.P., privately printed, 1912.

Athey, Lou, *Kaymoor: A New River Community*. Oak Hill, West Virginia: Eastern National Park & Monument Association, 1986.

Athey, Lou, "The Low Moor Iron Company of Virginia, 1873-1930," *Proceedings*, New River Symposium, April 10-12, 1986, Wytheville, Virginia, pp. 141-50.

Bias, Charles, "Building the Chesapeake and Ohio Railroad Through the New River Region," *Proceedings*, New River Symposium, May 6-8, 1982, Beckley, West Virginia, pp. 168-175.

Bias, Charles, "The Completion of the Chesapeake and Ohio Railroad to the Ohio River, 1869-1873," *West Virginia History*, XL, No. 4 (Summer 1979), pp. 393-403.

Cavalier, John, *Panorama of Fayette County*. Parsons, West Virginia: McClain Printing Company, 1985.

Chadwick, Douglas, "New River Towns: 1900-1920," *Goldenseal*, vol. 2, no. 2 (April-June 1976), pp. 17-39.

Chadwick, Douglas, "Nothing Will Ever Bring Them Back," *Goldenseal*, vol. 2, no. 1 (January-March 1976), pp. 35-42.

Conley, Phil, *History of the West Virginia Coal Industry*. Charleston, West Virginia: Education Foundation, 1960.

Dixon, Thomas W., Jr., "Foreword," *Chesapeake & Ohio Diesel Review*, pp. 4-5. Alderson, West Virginia: Chesapeake & Ohio Historical Society, 1982.

Donnelly, Shirley, *Historical Notes on Fayette County, W. Va*. No place given: privately printed, 1958.

Donnelly, Shirley, *The Thurmonds*. No place given: privately printed, c.1939.

Ernest, Dale S., "Thurmond, West Virignia -- My Boyhood Home Town," *Proceedings*, New River Symposium, April 10-12, 1986, Wytheville, Virginia, pp. 77-88.

Evans, Cerinda W., *Collis Potter Huntington*. Newport News, Virginia: The Mariners Museum, 1954. Volume 2.

Fayette County Deed Books G, 26, 27, 40, 41, 42.

Fayette County Register of Deaths, 1900-03.

Fayette Journal, Fayetteville, West Virginia.

Fayette Tribune, Fayetteville, West Virginia.

Fisk & Hatch, Bankers, *The Chesapeake and Ohio Railroad as a Short, Economical, and Profitable Line from the Atlantic Coast to the Great West*. New York: Privately published, 1871.

Frazier, Harry, *Recollections*. Huntington West Virginia: Chesapeake & Ohio Railway, 1938.

Lane, Ron and Ted Schnepf, *Sewell: A New River Community*. Oak Hill, West Virginia: Eastern National Park & Monument Association, 1985.

Lee, Howard B., *Bloodletting in Appalachia*. Morgantown: West Virginia University, 1969.

Massey, Tim R., "Remembering Bill McKell," *Goldenseal*, vol. 8, no. 3 (Fall 1982), pp. 20-21.

McCormick, Kyle, *The New-Kanawha River and the Mine Wars of West Virginia.* Charleston: Mathews Printing Co., 1959.

Miller, Thomas Condit, and Hu Maxwell, *West Virginia and Its People.* New York: Lewis Historical Publishing Co., 1913. Volume 2.

National Park Service, New River Gorge National River Collection. Oak Hill, West Virginia:

General Management Plan: New River Gorge National River, West Virginia. Denver: National Park Service Denver Service Center, 1982.

Paul D. Marshall and Associates, *A Cultural Research Project: New River Gorge National River, West Virginia.* Charleston, West Virginia: Paul D. Marshall and Associates, 1981.

Oral History Transcripts, National Park Service:
Wallace Roscoe Bennett. Oak Hill, West Virginia. Interview. October 1, 1980.
Virginia Gray. Glen Jean, West Virginia. Interview. July 13, 1985.
William Harris. Stansford, West Virginia. Interview. July 13, 1985.
Jack Kelly. Thurmond, West Virginia. Interview. July 13, 1985.
Jane Graham Lawson. Oak Hill, West Virginia. Interview. November 5, 1980.
Roy C. Long. Hinton, West Virginia. Interview. July 13, 1985.
Herman Monk. Beckley, West Virginia. Interview. August 17, 1980.
Jacqueline Pugh. Thurmond, West Virignia. Interview. July 6, 1985.
John Richmond. Pipestem, West Virginia. Interview. July 26, 1985.
Carlton B. Webb. Pleasant Hill, California. Self-interview. No date.

Peters, J. T., and H. B. Carden, *History of Fayette County, West Virginia.* Charleston, West Virginia: Jarrett Printing Company, 1926.

R. L. Polk & Co., *West Virginia State Gazetteer and Business Directory,* annual and biennial volumes, 1895-96 to 1912-13.

Scott, Eugene Lewis, *Thurmond: Dodge City of West Virginia: Believe It or Not City.* N.P., privately printed, n.d.

Scott, Eugene Lewis, "Thurmond on the New River," *West Virginia Review,* vol. 23, no. 5 (February 1946), pp. 22-24, pp. 45-46; vol. 23, no. 6 (March 1946), pp. 20-22; vol. 23, no. 7 (April 1946), pp. 10-12; vol. 23, no. 8 (May 1946), pp. 12-15.

Sullivan, Charles Kenneth, "Coal Men and Coal Towns: Development of the Smokeless Coalfields of Southern West Virginia, 1873-1923." Unpublished Ph.D. dissertation, University of Pittsburgh, 1979.

Tams, W. P., Jr., *The Smokeless Coal Fields of West Virginia: A Brief History.* Morgantown, West Virginia: West Virginia University Library, 1963.

Thurmond, Walter R., "The Town of Thurmond, 1884-1961," *West Virginia History,* XXII, No. 4 (July 1961), pp. 240-54.

U.S., Census Office, 10th Census, 1880. *Report on the Mining Industries of the United States,* by Raphael Pumpelly. Washington: Government Printing Office, 1886.

U.S., Census Office, 13th Census, 1910. Manuscript population returns.

Witschey, Walter R. T., "Smokin' Guns and Smokeless Coal: Thurmond, West Virginia: New River Boom Town," *Proceedings,* New River Symposium, April 14-16, 1983, Blacksburg, Virginia, pp. 9-13.

Witschey, Walter R. T., *The Thurmonds of Virginia.* Richmond: The Gatewood Company, 1978.